BECOME AN ENTREPRENEUR

Business, Leadership & More

Carla Mooney

An imprint of Abdo Publishing
abdobooks.com

ABDOBOOKS.COM

Published by Abdo Publishing, a division of ABDO, PO Box 398166, Minneapolis, Minnesota 55439.

Printed in the United States of America, North Mankato, Minnesota
102024
012025

Design: Denise Hamernik, Mighty Media, Inc.
Production: Mighty Media, Inc.
Editor: Katherine Chu

Cover Photographs: Adobe Stock (calendar, notebook); Shutterstock Images (binder clips, cord, desk background, laptop, paper clips, payment machine, pencil, pile of reports, shanking hands, smartphones, tablet)

Interior Photographs: Adobe Stock, pp. 10 (top middle, bottom left), 10–11, 11 (bottom), 44 (all), 45 (all), 46–47 (background), 47 (all); Edward Dodwell/Wikimedia Commons, p. 6 (bottom); Mighty Media, Inc. (project photos), pp. 50, 51; Richard Cantillon/Wikimedia Commons, p. 9 (top); Shutterstock Images, pp. 3, 4, 5 (all), 6 (top), 8, 9 (bottom), 10 (top left), 11 (top), 12, 13 (all), 14 (all), 15, 16 (all), 17, 18, 19, 20 (all), 21 (all), 22 (all), 23 (all), 24 (all), 25 (all), 26, 27 (all), 28 (all), 29, 30 (all), 31 (all), 32 (all), 33 (all), 34 (all), 35 (all), 36, 37, 38 (all), 39 (all), 40, 41, 42 (all), 43 (all), 46 (right), 48 (all), 48–49 (background), 50–51 (background), 52, 53, 54, 56, 57, 58 (all), 59, 60, 61 (all); Sipa USA/Alamy Photo, p. 55

Design Elements: Adobe Stock (Polaroid frame, sticky notes, tacks); Shutterstock Images (calculator texture, crumpled paper texture, money texture)

The following names appearing in this book are trademarks: Excel®, PowerPoint®, Windows®, Word®

Library of Congress Control Number: 2024938224

PUBLISHER'S CATALOGING-IN-PUBLICATION DATA

Names: Mooney, Carla, author.
Title: Become an entrepreneur: business, leadership & more/ by Carla Mooney
Other Title: business, leadership and more
Description: Minneapolis, Minnesota : ABDO Publishing, 2025 | Series: Talent to trade | Includes online resources and index.
Identifiers: ISBN 9781098294946 (lib. bdg.) | ISBN 9798384914990 (ebook)
Subjects: LCSH: Business management--Juvenile literature. | Budget in business--Juvenile literature. | Entrepreneurs--Juvenile literature. | Small businesses--Juvenile literature. | Jobs--Juvenile literature. | Trades--Juvenile literature.
Classification: DDC 650.14--dc23

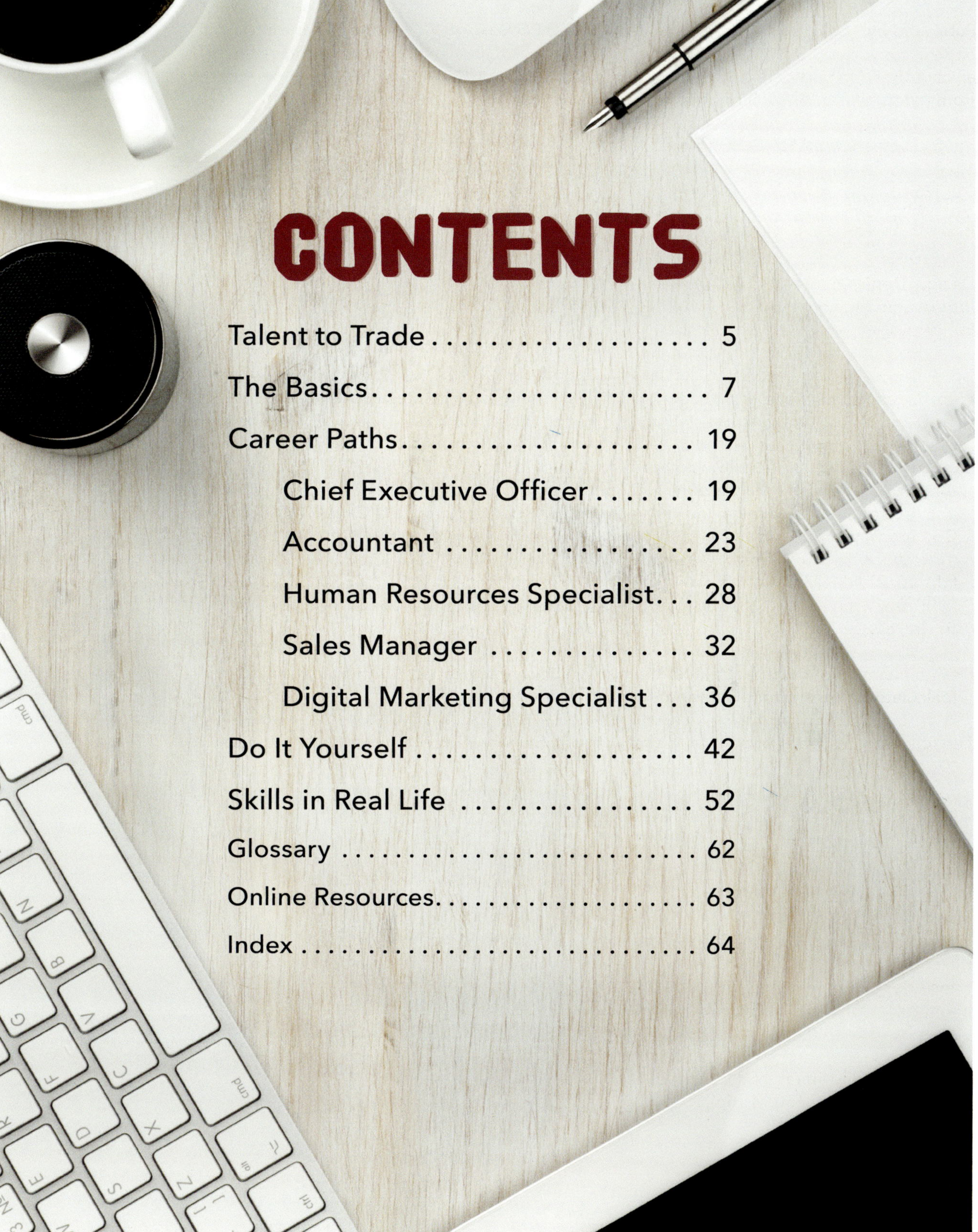

CONTENTS

TALENT TO TRADE

Do entrepreneurs fascinate you? Can you see yourself working in management, accounting, or marketing? Do you dream of starting your own business? If your answer to any of these questions is yes, you might be suited to a career as an entrepreneur. This is a person who starts or owns a business.

Becoming an entrepreneur takes a lot of training and hard work. It takes dedication to mastering business skills, following business trends, and satisfying customers. But if you have a passion for business, you may find that the dedication comes naturally and the hard work is worthwhile.

In this book, you'll learn about the history of entrepreneurship and various jobs in the business industry. You'll become familiar with some basic business tools, skills, and techniques. You'll find inspiration to begin working toward your career in business or as an entrepreneur. Finally, you'll learn about some of the ways you can turn your talents into a trade.

Many societies in ancient China used cowrie shells as money.

Markets are located everywhere around the world. In the Middle East, they are known as *souks*. In Iran, they are *bazaars* (*pictured*). And markets are called *palengke* in the Philippines.

HISTORY OF ENTREPRENEURSHIP

The word *entrepreneur* comes from the French word *entreprendre,* which means "to undertake." Entrepreneurs create products and services that change the way people live. They also start businesses or companies based on their ideas.

Entrepreneurship has been around since ancient civilization. In the beginning, ancient people bartered with one another. They traded goods and services for other goods and services. For example, a person who grew crops traded with a neighbor who made medicines. The barter system worked because it depended on each person having something someone else needed.

Soon, ancient people began to use a different system to exchange goods and services: money. Money helped people assign a value to something. With money, they could exchange goods of the same value. Ancient people first used rocks, shells, or other small items as money. One of the first uses of money was in ancient China around 1200 BCE. Over time, money became pieces of metal and, eventually, gold.

As early communities grew, people specialized in tasks such as making jewelry or growing crops. As people traded specialized goods and services with one another for money, entrepreneurship began to take hold. People traveled farther for goods and services they couldn't get from their own communities. And, communities established markets where people would gather to buy goods and services. People called traders began moving goods between communities. They traveled regular routes, known as trade routes, transporting goods from market to market.

In the late 1700s and early 1800s, the Industrial Revolution occurred. People invented new machines and manufacturing processes. This led to permanent changes in the way people lived and worked. New machines powered industrial factories. Products that used to take days or weeks to make could now be produced in hours. Cities grew as people from rural communities moved close to factories and took factory jobs. And the invention of the steam engine led to the rise of railroads. Goods could now be carried across longer distances. As demand and production increased, entrepreneurs grew larger businesses. And, people were able to offer their business knowledge and services to help companies succeed.

Advancing technology and the discovery of new energy sources led to a new wave of entrepreneurs. These entrepreneurs created many life-changing inventions still used today. In 1876, Alexander Graham Bell invented the electric telephone. In 1880, Thomas Edison patented the first electric light bulb. In 1903, brothers Orville and Wilbur Wright made their first successful flight on an airplane. And in 1908, Henry Ford created the Model T, an affordable vehicle for the average person. But these people were not just inventors. They also started companies to manufacture and sell their inventions. And as their companies grew, they hired different types of employees to help their businesses run smoothly. These included accountants, human resources (HR) specialists, sales managers, digital marketing specialists, and more. Some entrepreneurs also employed a chief executive officer (CEO) to manage and run the entire company.

Modern entrepreneurs have developed computers, cell phones, wireless technology, and more. Steve Jobs was one of the world's

English engineer George Stephenson created the Rocket. This was the first commercial steam engine to work on rails.

best-known modern entrepreneurs. Jobs co-founded Apple, Inc. Apple has created products such as the Apple computer, iPod, iPhone, iPad, and Apple watch. These devices have revolutionized how people use computers, keep in touch, listen to music, and more. Apple also employs many business professionals who work hard to keep the company successful.

Today, there are more than 582 million entrepreneurs worldwide. In the following pages, you'll learn what it takes to work in business and as an entrepreneur. You may even be inspired to start your journey to becoming an entrepreneur or business professional!

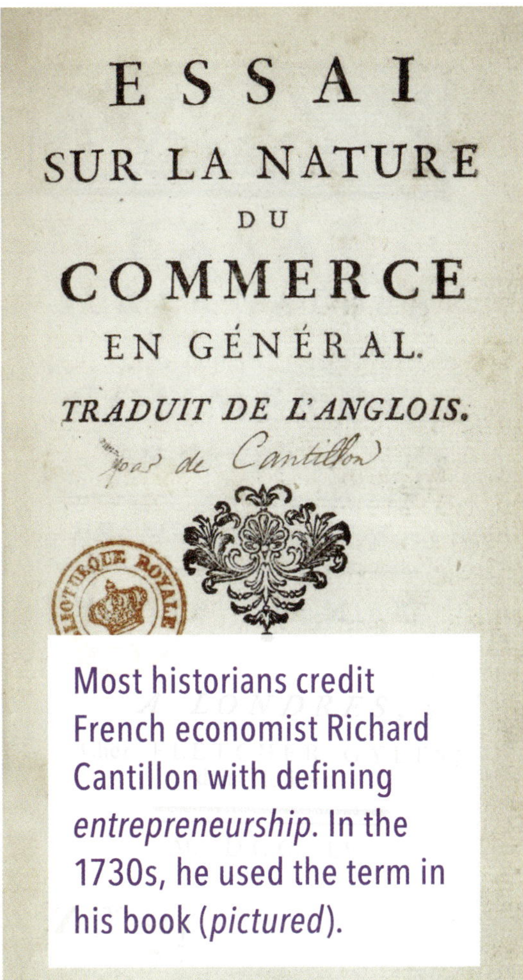

ESSAI
SUR LA NATURE
DU
COMMERCE
EN GÉNÉRAL.
TRADUIT DE L'ANGLOIS.

Most historians credit French economist Richard Cantillon with defining *entrepreneurship*. In the 1730s, he used the term in his book (*pictured*).

Social media influencers are often modern entrepreneurs. Many start their own businesses from the brand they create online.

TOOLS OF THE TRADE

Get familiar with some of the tools entrepreneurs use day-to-day in business.

COMPUTER

Many entrepreneurs use computers to create new products and services. These include laptops, desktops, and tablets. No matter the type, computers are used in almost every part of a business's operations. They are used to communicate, store information, analyze data, and more. For example, CEOs use computers to research trends, identify potential customers, and learn about competitors. Computers help digital marketing specialists create media, such as graphics or videos. And HR specialists use computers to manage payroll systems and employee records.

COMPUTER PROGRAMS

Business professionals use different computer programs to complete their many tasks. Word processing programs create text documents. Spreadsheet programs organize and store data in rows and columns. Users can search, sort, and calculate spreadsheet data in various ways. Presentation programs can easily create slideshow presentations. And design programs help create and develop products.

Every business professional uses software programs to help them be efficient. Accountants use programs to send and receive payments, track revenue and expenses, and pay taxes. Time-keeping software helps HR specialists track employee work hours. Digital marketing specialists use programs to create and maintain websites. And many professionals use project management software to organize and track their projects' progress.

CALCULATOR

The job of every entrepreneur involves numbers at some point. For example, they might have to add items on a customer invoice or calculate taxes. A calculator can quickly perform most of the calculations that an entrepreneur will need to do.

SMARTPHONE

With a smartphone, business professionals can communicate with employees, customers, and vendors from almost anywhere. But smartphones are much more than communication devices. They are powerful handheld computers. Professionals use smartphones to do online banking, make purchases, research information, and more.

SPECIAL SKILLS

Explore some of the skills that entrepreneurs need to do their jobs.

ANALYTICS

Entrepreneurs gather, collect, and analyze data from many sources. This data may relate to finances, operations, marketing, sales, competitors, and more. Entrepreneurs must organize, understand, and make connections between different pieces of data. Then they use this analysis to strategize and make decisions so their business can achieve its goals.

To be successful, all business professionals need to be analytical. CEOs analyze financial data and other business metrics to make high-level company decisions. Accountants evaluate financial data, identify problems, and suggest solutions. Sales managers and digital marketing specialists analyze sales data and online metrics. This helps them decide on strategies to attract customers.

BUSINESS KNOWLEDGE

All entrepreneurs plan, organize and direct a business's operations and resources. A person with business knowledge, sometimes called business sense, understands the issues and situations an organization could face. They make decisions to help their business succeed and meet goals. It is especially important that CEOs have business knowledge, as they run and manage companies. HR specialists also use this skill to ensure their company follows all laws and regulations.

INTERPERSONAL COMMUNICATION

Entrepreneurs run a business, build and maintain relationships, understand needs, and make decisions. They must be able to explain ideas clearly, listen effectively, answer questions, and show empathy. They must also be comfortable interacting with people of all backgrounds and experiences. This is because they communicate daily with customers, vendors, employees, and investors. For example, an entrepreneur may have an exciting idea for a new product. But if they cannot communicate the idea effectively, it won't be easy to convince others to invest in their business or purchase their product.

For business professionals, strong communication and interpersonal skills are essential. CEOs frequently interact with the public, employees, customers, and others. They also negotiate and explain policies and procedures to people inside and outside the company. Accountants frequently discuss their findings with clients, executives, and co-workers. HR specialists work with job applicants, employees, and managers. Sales managers must make sales and address customers' questions and concerns. And digital marketing specialists need strong writing skills to create blog posts, website articles, and other online content. They also engage others online through email and social media.

CREATIVITY

Entrepreneurs think creatively to develop and build their businesses. They brainstorm and evaluate new ways to create products that meet customer needs. HR specialists need to be creative in finding ways to recruit new employees. Digital marketing specialists create engaging content to attract new customers and retain existing ones.

FINANCIAL MANAGEMENT

Most entrepreneurs sell products or services, collect payments, and pay vendors. They need to track revenue and expenses and keep detailed financial records. They may also have to prepare financial statements, budgets, and forecasts. A company may hire one or more accountants to help manage these financial tasks. But business owners must understand how their finances were prepared. And CEOs must analyze financial reports to understand what factors impact a company's cash flow. They use these reports to make decisions that increase profits and reduce losses.

Entrepreneurs design products and services to meet the needs of their target market. Marketing is also an essential skill for digital marketing specialists. They create a company's brand, interact with potential customers, and engage with social media users.

LEADERSHIP

Entrepreneurs inspire employees of all backgrounds and experience levels. Good leaders understand their employees' motivations. They strive to meet employees' needs and create a positive working environment. Any business professional who manages employees also needs to lead and guide them. CEOs must lead their company and give clear directions for managers to implement. And sales managers often lead a sales team. They evaluate their employees' performance and help them achieve sales goals.

MARKETING

Entrepreneurs market their products and services to customers. Important marketing skills include identifying and analyzing a target market. This is the group of people who will most likely buy a company's products or services.

PROBLEM-SOLVING & DECISION-MAKING

Entrepreneurs deal with various issues, from supply shortages to unhappy customers. They must handle challenging situations and come up with solutions. Problem-solving and decision-making skills are valuable regardless of a person's job or experience level. CEOs assess situations and problems, identify solutions, and decide on the best actions to reach company goals. And HR specialists make decisions

as they review job applications and conduct interviews. They also problem-solve when resolving employees' issues.

STRATEGIC PLANNING

As entrepreneurs and business professionals handle everyday problems and decisions, they must also think strategically about the future. CEOs create plans for employees to follow. This helps companies grow and meet their long-term goals. And sales managers create sales strategies that set their companies apart from competitors.

TIME MANAGEMENT

Entrepreneurs juggle many tasks simultaneously. They need to manage their time wisely to execute projects from start to finish. Entrepreneurs also need to know how to prioritize and delegate tasks. Many business professionals need to be efficient and organized to stay on top of their tasks. CEOs prioritize tasks to ensure their companies meet their goals. Accountants often manage multiple tasks, clients, and deadlines. And HR specialists manage both applicants and employees.

CAREERS IN BUSINESS

An entrepreneur works hard to establish their business or company. And as their company grows, they may decide to hire business professionals to help it run efficiently. These business professionals perform a wide range of tasks across various industries. However, many business professionals choose to specialize in one area of business. Let's explore some career paths for those interested in business!

CHIEF EXECUTIVE OFFICER

As an entrepreneur's company grows and becomes more established, they may hire a CEO to run and manage it. The CEO is the highest-ranking employee in any business. They are responsible for setting a business's direction, strategizing, and managing a team of employees to achieve business goals.

MANAGING OPERATIONS

A CEO's main objective is to make sure the company they manage runs smoothly. They also negotiate and sign contracts for the business. A CEO's responsibilities depend on the size of the business. In small businesses, CEOs are usually more involved in daily operations. They tend to take on multiple roles. These include anything from sales and customer service representative to hiring manager to employee trainer. In larger businesses, CEOs usually delegate some responsibilities to other managers and employees.

SETTING GOALS

In larger businesses, CEOs spend more time setting company goals. They also develop strategies to meet those goals. Most CEOs have a long-term vision for the business. They work with other executives and managers to create and implement plans to achieve that vision. CEOs also guide their companies and ensure their employees follow long-term plans.

MONITORING PERFORMANCE

CEOs monitor their company's operations and performance to keep it on track to meet its goals. They do this by reviewing financial statements, sales reports, and other business data. CEOs may also travel to customers or company sites to monitor performance and progress. This helps CEOs make major decisions for the business. They also use the data to identify how they might reduce expenses or adjust plans if necessary.

PUBLIC RELATIONS

A CEO is often the face of a company. They publicly share major business changes or present the launch of new products or services. They may do this by issuing a press release. This is a written or recorded statement CEOs present to the public. CEOs also represent their companies at events. They may speak at conferences, attend community gatherings and more.

CEOs work closely with managers to monitor and evaluate employee performance.

CEOs share goals and progress with shareholders. These are people who have invested in the company.

Accountants check financial statements for fraud.

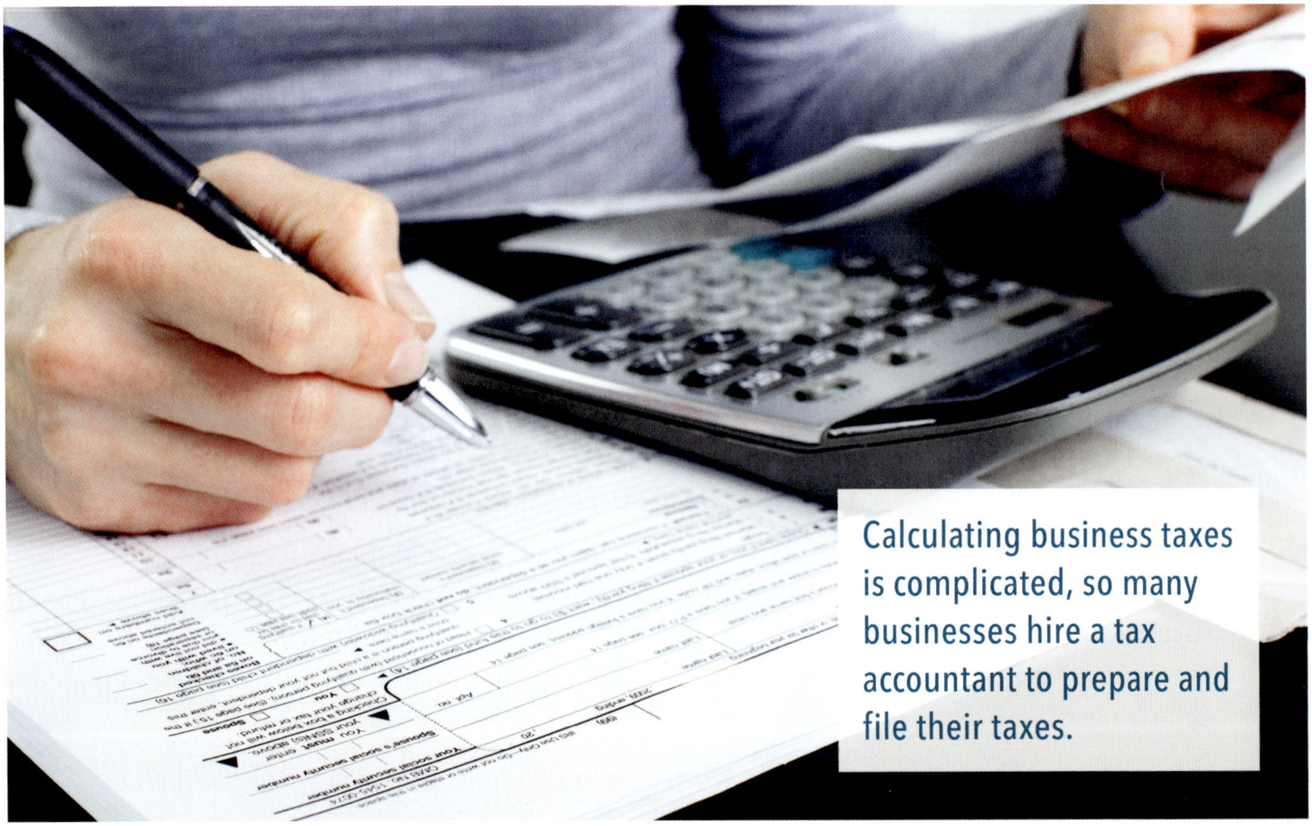

Calculating business taxes is complicated, so many businesses hire a tax accountant to prepare and file their taxes.

ACCOUNTANT

As an entrepreneur's business grows, they usually hire one or more accountants to keep their finances in order. Accountants prepare and analyze financial records. They do this for all types of businesses, industries, and individuals. They ensure that financial records are accurate. They also help businesses identify risks and opportunities.

FINANCIAL RECORDS

Accountants prepare and review financial statements. They follow procedures known as the generally accepted accounting principles. This is the process every accountant follows to ensure statements are prepared correctly. When doing this, they must pay attention to every detail. This includes making sure financial statements meet all laws and regulations. Accountants also set up and maintain accounting computer systems. They must correctly enter all transactions into the appropriate system.

BILLING & COLLECTIONS

Part of an accountant's job is to maintain sales and payment records. They send invoices to customers and make sure customer accounts are paid on time. Accountants must also maintain purchase records and make payments to vendors. Additionally, accountants calculate federal, state, and other business taxes. They prepare tax returns and ensure all taxes are paid on time.

FINANCIAL ANALYSIS

Accountants analyze financial information. They assess a business's financial performance and identify any risks it may face. For example, an accountant reviewing a company's records may notice a customer is far behind on payments. The accountant may recommend the company stop sales to the customer until the account is paid in full. This limits the financial risk the company faces if the customer never pays.

PREPARING REPORTS

Accountants prepare financial reports to help executives, such as a CEO. For example, they may create budgets and forecasts. Then accountants compare these with the actual costs. They explain their findings in a report for executives to review. Executives use these reports to make informed decisions for the business.

MANAGEMENT ACCOUNTANTS

Accountants that prepare internal financial reports for a company's executives and managers are called management or corporate accountants. Some management accountants specialize in specific areas of accounting. This can include accounts payable. This is the money a company pays to those who sell them supplies or equipment. Accountants might also work collections, which is the money a company collects from customers. Or they may work in budgeting, where they help create a plan of future expenses. Other accountants specialize in a specific industry such as finance, healthcare, or manufacturing.

Accountants can make suggestions to raise sales, reduce costs, and increase profits.

A forecast is a prediction of future costs based on past data.

Accountants may advise companies on financial performance and management.

GOVERNMENT ACCOUNTANTS

Some accountants work for federal, state, or local governments. They maintain and review the accounting records of government agencies. They also make sure these government agencies are following laws and regulations. Some government accountants review the accounting records of private companies and individuals for the government. For example, government accountants for the Internal Revenue Service review private individual tax returns.

PUBLIC ACCOUNTANTS

Many accountants work for public accounting firms or have their own businesses. They provide accounting, auditing, tax, and consulting services. Their clients include individuals, businesses, companies, and nonprofit organizations. Sometimes the law requires companies to publicize certain financial statements. Some public accountants audit these statements. Other public accountants prepare tax returns or advise clients on tax matters. Public accountants also provide advice on personal investments and financial planning. And some public accountants, called forensic accountants, investigate fraud and other financial crimes.

HUMAN RESOURCES SPECIALIST

As a business or company grows, so does the number of employees. Companies may have an HR specialist hire and manage employees. An HR specialist's responsibilities involve recruiting and training new employees, managing compensation and benefits, and more.

HIRING EMPLOYEES

HR specialists handle all the tasks of managing a company's employees. They work with executives and managers to determine if the business needs new employees. If a company needs to hire new employees, HR specialists advertise open positions and recruit job applicants. They also manage applicants throughout the interview process. This means they communicate with applicants, review resumes, check references, and run background checks. Many HR specialists will conduct initial interviews to determine if applicants are a good fit. They explain job details, such as duties and benefits, to applicants. They may also schedule applicants' interviews with managers and executives. Additionally, HR specialists often work with managers and executives to select and hire new employees.

HR specialists manage the forms and documents new employees read and sign. These include employee agreements, tax forms, benefit plans, and more.

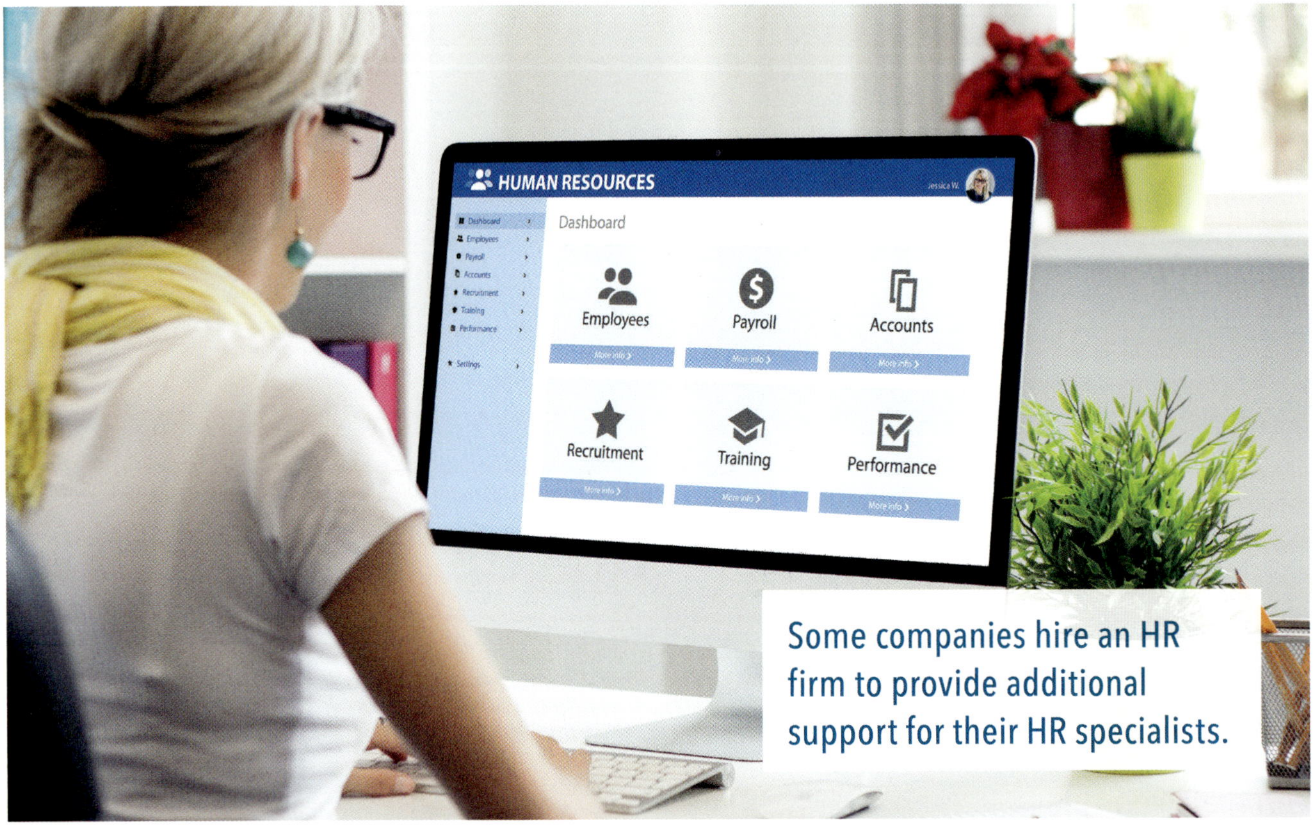

Some companies hire an HR firm to provide additional support for their HR specialists.

Recruitment specialists often attend job fairs and visit college campuses.

ORIENTATION

Once employees are hired, HR specialists often perform new employee orientation. During orientation, they ensure new employees complete all required paperwork. They set up new employees in company systems, enroll them in payroll and benefits, and issue identification badges. Sometimes, HR specialists also conduct training for new employees.

PAYROLL TO POLICIES

HR specialists maintain a company's employment records. They process payroll and administer benefits for all employees. HR specialists maintain a company's policy and procedure manuals. They also answer employees' questions about company policies. And, they ensure all HR records and operations meet federal, state, and local regulations.

SPECIALIZATION

Some HR specialists perform all HR tasks for a company. Larger companies may hire a team of HR specialists. Each specialist in the team performs a specific task, such as recruiting or training. For example, a recruitment specialist's entire job revolves around finding qualified employees. They post new job listings, research potential candidates, and more. A training specialist focuses exclusively on planning and conducting training programs. They work to improve employees' skills and knowledge.

SALES MANAGER

An entrepreneur may hire a sales manager to help sell their company's products or services. Sales managers identify new customers. They also maintain relationships with existing customers. Some sales managers deal with sales to other businesses. Others focus on direct sales to individual customers. Managers might also lead a team of sales representatives.

PRODUCTS & SERVICES

A sales manager's responsibilities vary from business to business. In most companies, managers are responsible for selling products or services to customers. They identify potential customers and follow leads from existing customers. Managers explain the benefits and features of the product or service to customers. Then they answer questions and negotiate prices. They also work to maintain customer relationships and address any concerns.

MANAGING A TEAM

In large companies, sales managers may lead a sales team. Managers take part in the process to recruit, hire, and train new sales representatives. They set goals for individual sales representatives. To reach these goals, managers meet with sales representatives and give suggestions on improving performance. Managers also conduct ongoing training for the sales team.

Sales managers often attend trade shows and conferences to find new customers.

Managers assign representatives to different sales territories, or geographical areas. This helps divide responsibilities, organize sales, and increase productivity.

Sales data helps managers decide the price of products, when to have promotions, and more.

A sales manager may work closely with the product development team to understand a product. This helps them sell the product and answer customers' questions.

ANALYZING SALES DATA

Sales managers often analyze sales and customer data. This data helps them determine which products are selling and which are not. They use this information to understand what customers want. They may also use sales data to determine how much inventory a company needs to have.

WORKING WITH OTHER DEPARTMENTS

Sales managers work closely with other company departments. The marketing department might identify and send a lead, or potential new customer, to the sales manager. The sales manager would then contact the lead or delegate this task to one of their sales representatives. Sales managers work closely with product development teams to ensure customers' preferences are considered in product designs. Managers also work with warehouse departments to manage inventory levels. Working with other departments can bring new insights that help sales managers make decisions.

DIGITAL MARKETING SPECIALIST

Another way entrepreneurs can help grow their company or business is by hiring a digital marketing specialist. These specialists create marketing campaigns, activities that promote products and services. Marketing specialists launch campaigns through various digital channels, such as company websites, social media, email, and blogs. They also post and update all other digital content as well as monitor its performance. This means they analyze how their audience interacts with the content they create. These specialists also ensure their content aligns with their marketing objectives. They work alongside content creators who assist in making marketable content. These creators may include graphic designers, video editors, and others.

BUILDING A BRAND

A digital marketing specialist's goal is to attract new customers and increase a company's brand awareness. Brand awareness is how familiar the public is with a company and its products or services. Specialists increase brand awareness by creating a variety of compelling content. This includes articles, videos, podcasts, social media posts, and more.

Some digital marketers create their own content.

Digital marketing specialists may work with social media influencers to promote a company's products or services.

Websites include information that can educate customers and answer questions they may have about a company's products or services.

COMPANY WEBSITE

Digital marketing specialists use a company's website to attract and engage users. They create interesting and valuable content that appeals to a company's target customer base. This content includes articles, blog posts, and more.

SOCIAL MEDIA

Companies can reach millions of potential customers through social media sites and applications. Digital marketing specialists create content for various social media platforms. They post and monitor content to see how well it does. They interact with social media users and respond to any questions they have. And they stay on top of social media trends to make sure their content stays relevant.

EMAIL CAMPAIGNS

Digital marketing specialists also use email to connect with both potential and current customers. Emails are used to inform people of the latest company and product news. This can increase customer engagement with a brand. It can be a way to reach new customers as well as build positive relationships with existing ones.

SEARCH ENGINE OPTIMIZATION

Search engine optimization (SEO) is the strategy of boosting a website's ranking on search engines such as Google. This can help bring more customers to the company website. Digital marketing specialists research words and phrases that potential customers might use in search engines. They include these words and phrases in their online content. They also create and use other strategies to drive more search engine results to their website.

MARKETING ANALYTICS

Digital marketing specialists gather data on their digital marketing campaigns. This includes tracking website visitors, social media views, and other online metrics. Specialists review how many people visit the company's website and where they are from. They also look at which content generates the most engagement. They analyze this data to determine how successful each marketing campaign is. The data helps them improve their strategies and create effective marketing campaigns.

Specialists sometimes collect data shared by similar companies or data collected and sold by other organizations. This can help a specialist improve their marketing tactics.

CREATE YOUR VISION

It's time to get creative! Think about your hobbies and interests that relate to business and entrepreneurship. Create a vision board that reflects these and whatever else inspires you. Let it motivate you to turn your talents into your trade!

Put your vision board where you'll see it on a regular basis, such as in your locker or next to your bed.

"Genius is 1% inspiration and 99% perspiration."
– Thomas Edison

"Your most unhappy customers are your greatest source of learning."
— Bill Gates
Rihanna
Selena Gomez
Display magazine pages, quotes, and photos of entrepreneurs who inspire you.
Create a list of business ideas, things to do, and goals. Add notes or make a sample schedule.
My Goals
1
2
3
4
5

BRAINSTORM YOUR BUSINESS

You've got the passion, vision, and motivation. Even if you aren't ready to create your own business, you can start thinking about the types of businesses that would be a good fit!

Evaluate your strengths and interests. What do you like to do? What are you good at doing?

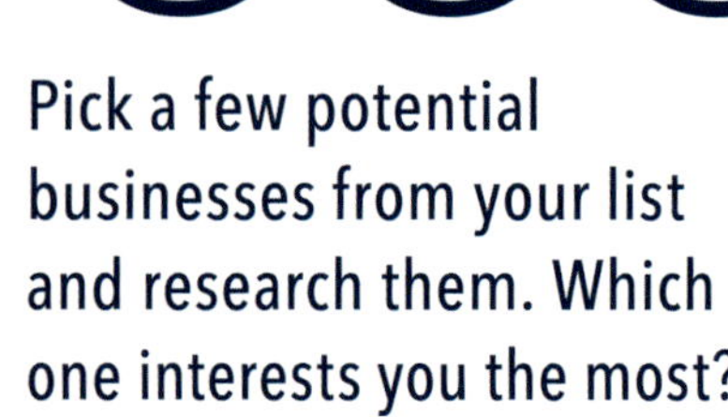

Pick a few potential businesses from your list and research them. Which one interests you the most?

Idea
Build a list of businesses that would be suited to your identified strengths and interests.
1
2
3

CREATE YOUR BUSINESS PLAN

Once you have an idea for a business, you need a plan! Entrepreneurs create business plans to help them get started. A business plan is a written document that describes your idea for a product or service. It explains how you plan to market the product or service. It also includes estimates of sales, expenses, and profits.

Making a business plan can help you decide if your idea is worth developing. Spending time on the plan now can save time and money later. As your business grows, investors and lenders will want to see your business plan to decide whether to invest in or lend money to your business.

Writing a business plan may seem challenging, but it can be as simple or complicated as you want!

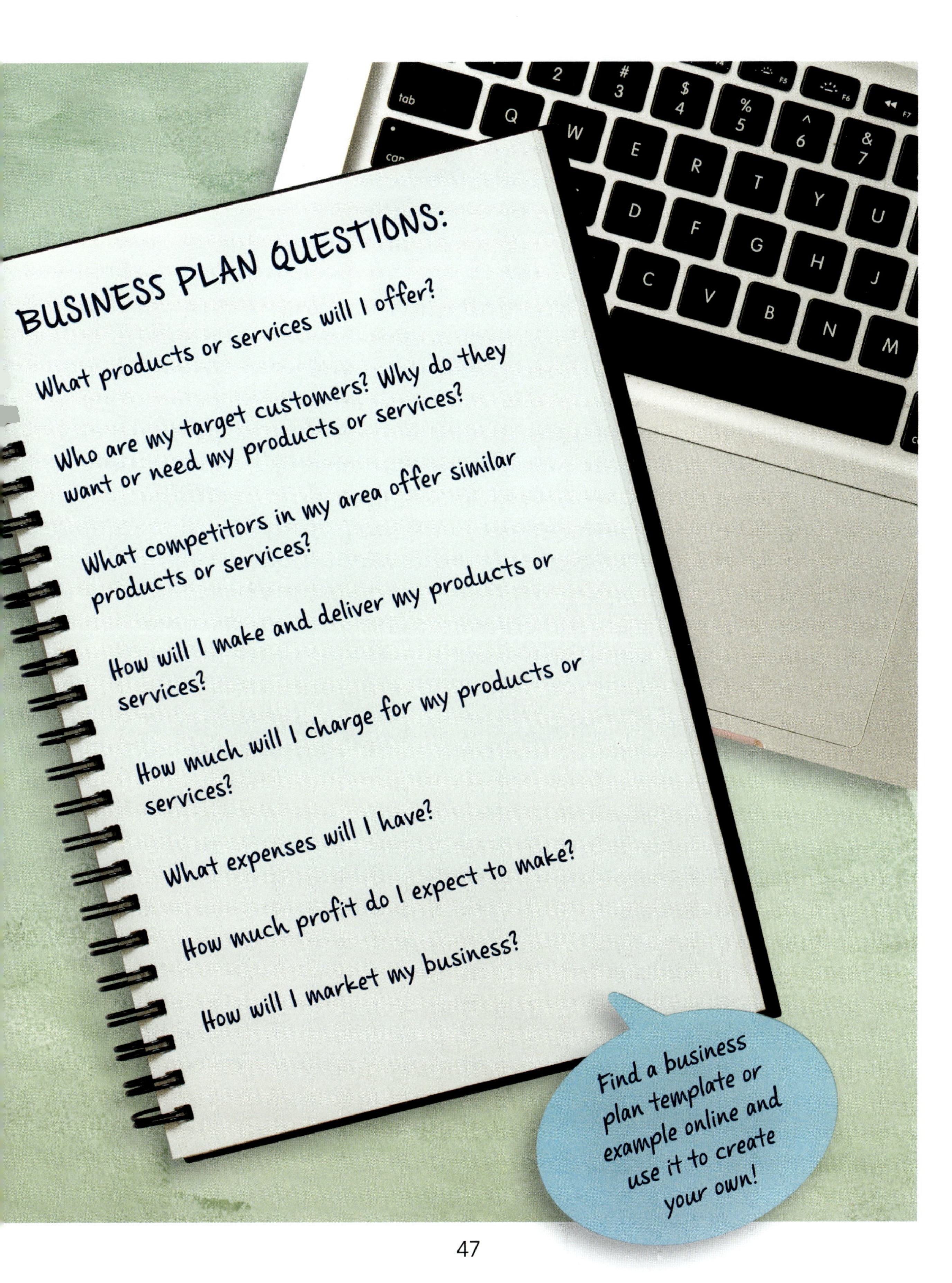
BUSINESS PLAN QUESTIONS:
What products or services will I offer?
Who are my target customers? Why do they want or need my products or services?
What competitors in my area offer similar products or services?
How will I make and deliver my products or services?
How much will I charge for my products or services?
What expenses will I have?
How much profit do I expect to make?
How will I market my business?
Find a business plan template or example online and use it to create your own!

EXPAND YOUR SKILLS

You have a great business plan. Now it's time to market your business and learn about finances. Marketing helps customers learn about your products or services. And getting experience with money will prepare you to handle your business's finances!

Volunteer to be the treasurer of a school club or fundraiser.

Join your school's Future Business Leaders of America (or similar) club.

Market your business through a website or social media.
BLOG

CREATE A CUSTOM FLYER

One way to market your product or service is by making a custom flyer!

SUPPLIES

paper
pencil
ruler
stencils (optional)
black permanent markers (different sizes)
photo
glue
colored markers (optional)
photocopier
tape or stapler

STEPS

1 Use a ruler and pencil to draw lines on the paper. This will help keep your words and design straight. Plan out the placement for a title, a photo, a brief message, and contact information. Consider adding a large graphic, such as a dog paw. Use stencils if you'd like.

2 Write your message in pencil to plan out the size, placement, and word choice. Consider making some important words block letters.

3 Once you are happy with your flyer, copy over your design with a thin black permanent marker. Add thicker lines to emphasize parts of your design. Erase all the pencil lines.

4 Add a creative border if there is room.

5 Attach a photo that represents your business, such as a picture of you with a dog. If you want, color in sections of the flyer to add more interest!

6 Make photocopies of the flyer.

7 Ask neighborhood shops if you can hang up your flyer in their space. Using tape or a stapler, hang flyers from lampposts where people will see them!

BECOMING AN ENTREPRENEUR

EDUCATION

Do you want to know what it takes to be an entrepreneur? Some people's path begins with a two-year or four-year college. Although you do not need a degree to become an entrepreneur, many people earn one. This allows them to study business concepts such as finance, marketing, accounting, and more.

Do you want to work for a company? Many companies require a bachelor's degree in a related field. Most accountants have a bachelor's degree in accounting or finance. Many HR specialists have a bachelor's degree in HR, communications, or business. And sales managers usually have a bachelor's degree in business, communications, or marketing.

Some companies also hire entry-level employees with a high school diploma or an associate's degree in a related field. They may also promote current employees with similar skills and experience. For example, an accountant with an associate's degree may start in an entry-level position and be promoted based on their performance. Some employers may prefer hiring applicants with previous work experience in a business field. For example, some digital marketing specialists have experience in print marketing, copywriting, content creation, web design, or similar fields.

Those interested in becoming entrepreneurs or working as business professionals may also get certified. Certificate programs provide specific training in specialized areas of business. These can include accounting, finance, digital marketing, and more. For example, many accountants earn certifications, such as Certified Public Accountant. There are also several HR associations that offer certifications based on experience.

FINDING A JOB

You want to become a business professional, and you've met the educational requirements. Now, it's time to find a job!

JOB SEARCH TIPS

- Create a résumé that outlines your education and training as well as your work history. Even if you have not worked in the industry, highlight any extracurricular experiences where you applied skills that are relevant to the role you are pursuing. If you have a website, online portfolio, or social media account showcasing your work, include these links in your résumé.
- Keep in regular contact with the instructors and classmates from your educational program. They can help put you in touch with others in the industry. The goal is to grow your professional network and learn about possible job opportunities.
- Identify businesses where you would like to work. Introduce yourself to the manager and ask for an informational interview so you can learn more about their business. Express your interest in working there, and leave them with a copy of your résumé.
- If you are invited to interview for a job, be prepared! Before the interview, research the business's history, mission statements, and offerings. Be ready to articulate why you want to work for the business and how you think you'd be a good fit for the role. Finally, have your own questions prepared for the interviewer. This shows you are thoughtful and serious about the job!
- Is there somewhere you really want to work, but there aren't any job openings for the role you're after? Consider applying for a different role, such as an intern or other entry-level position. This tactic is known as "getting your foot in the door." Using this tactic, you'll be in a solid position to be considered for your desired position when it becomes available.

CAREER PROGRESSION

Education does not stop once you land your first job. Even after entrepreneurs and business professionals are established in their careers, they should stay updated on the latest business trends as well as company and industry news. They take additional courses to earn certifications, attend industry conferences, and continue learning on the job. Continuing education helps entrepreneurs keep their skills sharp and prepares them for the next challenge.

Continuing education can help entrepreneurs increase their understanding of finance, marketing, strategy, and operations. It can also help them meet other professionals in the industry.

MEET A PRO: ERIC YUAN, ZOOM FOUNDER

Eric Yuan was born in China in 1970. Yuan moved to the United States after listening to Bill Gates give a speech about the growing internet industry. In 1997, he landed a job at WebEx, a communications company. He eventually became the company's vice president of engineering.

Yuan was interested in developing a smartphone-friendly videoconferencing system that was easier to use than WebEx's current products. But when WebEx turned down his idea, Yuan quit his job in 2011 and started his own company. In August 2012, Yuan's new company, Zoom, released its first videoconferencing product.

In less than 12 months, Zoom had 1 million users. By December 2019, 10 million people used Zoom daily. And during the COVID-19 pandemic, the number of daily users skyrocketed to 300 million. Today, more than 750,000 companies use Zoom to connect employees no matter where they are located. In 2020, *Time* magazine named Yuan "Businessperson of the Year."

Eric Yuan at the 2023 Breakthrough Prize ceremony in Los Angeles, California

TRADES AT WORK

EARNING POTENTIAL

The US Bureau of Labor Statistics provides estimated wage ranges for most workers in any given job category. The average salaries below are from May 2023. While these estimates provide a sense of what you could expect to earn, actual salaries can vary greatly depending on where you work, your amount of experience, and any specialized skills you have.

GROW YOUR POTENTIAL

Whatever salary you start at, there are various ways to grow your earning potential throughout your career. Here are a few ways to boost your income while continuing to do what you love.

Look for leadership opportunities. Look for ways to demonstrate your leadership skills on the job. In time, you may be promoted to a supervisory role in which you guide less-experienced employees.

Become your own boss. You are typically limited to a set income when working for an employer. If you're self-employed, your earnings can increase with your experience and the success of your business. Self-employment may mean opening a brick-and-mortar shop. Other options requiring less financial investment can include working from home or providing services online.

JOB CATEGORY	ANNUAL SALARY
Top Executives	$131,000–$239,000
Accountants and Auditors	$63,000–$104,000
Human Resources Specialists	$52,000–$92,000
Sales Managers	$94,000–$197,000
Public Relations Specialists	$50,000–$92,000

Brainstorm related products or services. If your product or service is successful, come up with related products or services to sell to your customers. For example, if you have a dog-walking business, you could add pet-sitting services. If you get creative, you may discover multiple ways to grow your business!

FINANCIAL SMARTS

However you're making money, managing your finances wisely is important.

If you have an employer, you will receive a regular paycheck from them. This income will be your wages minus taxes. If your employer offers health insurance, retirement savings, or other benefits, those will also be deducted from your take-home pay. Financial experts recommend you put about 20 percent of each paycheck into savings and try to

keep an emergency fund with enough money to cover three to six months' worth of living expenses.

If you are self-employed, you will receive payments directly from your customers. You'll need to track this income and your business expenses, such as rent and supplies. Self-employed individuals must also pay their taxes, generally four times a year, since they don't have an employer withholding taxes from each paycheck. Business owners use the remaining profits to pay themselves and fund savings accounts for themselves and the business.

If you have employees, you must pay both yourself and your employees. You must also manage your company's payroll, employee benefits, business insurance, and more. This takes a lot of work and organization. But hiring employees can bring many benefits, such as new skills and increased profits. It can also give you more time to focus on growing the business.

If you own a business, you will need to pay various business taxes. There are federal, state, and local income taxes. There are also sales taxes and employer payroll taxes. Often, business owners work with tax accountants who calculate taxes owed and prepare and file the proper tax forms. That way, taxes are filed correctly and on time.

DO WHAT YOU LOVE!

Being an entrepreneur requires a lot of training and hard work. Finding success as an entrepreneur can take years of effort and a commitment to keep learning and improving skills. Many entrepreneurs find the time and effort are worth the rewards of providing products and services that customers need and want.

Maybe your goal is to work for a company. Maybe you have your sights set on starting your own business. Or perhaps you want a weekend side hustle to earn extra income. As long as you do what you love, you'll love what you do.

GLOSSARY

analyze–to examine something to find out what it is or what makes it work. Analysis is the examination of something to find out how it works.

articulate–to clearly and effectively express oneself.

audit–to review or check a business's or company's financial accounts.

efficient–able to produce a desired result, especially without wasting time or energy. Efficiently means to do a task in a way that does not waste time or energy.

empathy–the understanding and sharing of another person's feelings.

forensic–used in or relating to a court of law.

graphic–an image on the screen of a computer, TV, or other device.

human resources–a department that oversees the hiring, administration, and training of employees.

Industrial Revolution–a period in England from about 1750 to 1850. It marked the change from an agricultural to an industrial society.

Internal Revenue Service–a government agency that collects taxes and oversees and enforces tax laws.

investor–someone who gives money to a company in return for part of the company's profits.

invoice–a statement that lists goods or services, their price, and sales terms.

metrics–measurements used for analysis.

monitor–to watch, keep track of, or oversee.

negotiate–to work out an agreement about the terms of something.

network–an interconnected group of people or computers.

orientation–a program that introduces new people to a business or company.

payroll–the money paid by a company to its employees.

potential–capable of being or becoming, or something that could be.

prioritize–to list in order of importance.

simultaneously–at the same time.

software—the written programs used by a computer.

specialize—to develop expertise in a certain area, called a specialty. A person who does this is a specialist. Specialized means suited to a particular purpose or occupation.

tax return—a report sent to the government that includes any money earned and the taxes paid in a year.

transaction—an exchange of goods, services, or funds.

vendor—a person or company that sells something.

ONLINE RESOURCES

To learn more about trades in business and entrepreneurship, please visit **abdobooklinks.com** or scan this QR code. These links are routinely monitored and updated to provide the most current information available.

INDEX